Golf is a game whose aim is to hit a very small ball into an even smaller hole, with weapons singularly ill-designed for the purpose.

Sir Winston Churchill

A BOOK OF

GOLFING
QUOTATIONS

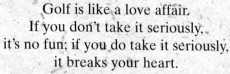

Golf is like a love affair.
If you don't take it seriously,
it's no fun; if you do take it seriously,
it breaks your heart.

Arnold Daly

All I have against it is that it takes you
so far from the clubhouse

Eric Linklater

Golf is a game in which a ball - one and
a half inches in diameter - is placed on a
ball - 8,000 miles in diameter.
The object being to hit the small ball,
but not the larger.

John Cunningham

If you watch a game, it's fun.
If you play it, it's recreation.
If you work at it, it's golf.

Bob Hope

Only religious ceremonies proceed with
more respect than the major golf
tournaments in this country.

Jimmy Cannon

You hit the ball and if it doesn't
go far enough you just hit it again,
and if that doesn't work, you hit it
again, and so on.

Robert Robinson

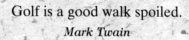

Golf is a good walk spoiled.

Mark Twain

He's hit it fat. . . . It will probably be
short. . . . It just hit the front edge of the
green. . . . It's got no chance. . . . It's
rolling but it will stop. . . . It's rolling
toward the cup. . . . Well, I'll be damned!

*Jimmy Demaret (commentating at the World
Championship in 1953 on Lew Worsham's
winning wedge shot)*

Golf is a fickle game,
and must be wooed to be won.

Willy Park Jr

A golf course is the epitome of all
that is purely transitory in the universe,
a space not to dwell in, but to get over
as quickly as possible.

Jean Giraudoux

There is one essential only in the golf
swing, the ball must be hit.

Sir Walter Simpson

I never pray on the golf course. Actually,
the Lord answers my prayers everywhere
except on the course.

Billy Graham

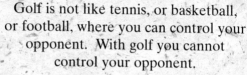

Golf is not like tennis, or basketball,
or football, where you can control your
opponent. With golf you cannot
control your opponent.

Tom Kite

At my first Masters, I got the feeling
that if I didn't play well, I wouldn't
go to heaven.

Dave Marr

I don't like doctors. They are like
golfers. Every one has a different
answer to your problem.

Severiano Ballesteros

My game is so bad I gotta hire three caddies - one to walk the left rough, one for the right rough, and one down the middle. And the one in the middle doesn't have much to do.

Dave Hill

When Nicklaus plays well he wins, when he plays badly he comes second. When he's playing terribly, he's third.

Johnny Miller

Golf is deceptively simple, endlessly complicated. A child can play it well and a grown man can never master it. It is almost a science, yet a puzzle with no answer.

Arnold Palmer

I have found, in my own matches, that if you just keep throwing consistent, unvarying bogeys and double bogeys at your opponents, they will crack up sooner or later from the pressure.

Rex Lardner

It's funny, but the more I practice, the luckier I become.

Gary Player

One reason golf is such an exasperating game is that a thing learned is so easily forgotten and we find ourselves struggling year after year with faults we had discovered and corrected time and time again.

Robert T. 'Bobby' Jones

My goal this year is basically to
find the fairways.

Lauri Peterson

My golf swing is like ironing a shirt.
You get one side smoothed out, turn it
over and there is a big wrinkle on the
other side. You iron that side, turn it
over and there's another wrinkle.

Tom Watson

The vital thing about a hole is that it
should either be more difficult than it
looks or look more difficult than it is.
It must never be what it looks.

Sir Walter Simpson

All games are silly, but golf, if you look
at it dispassionately, goes to extremes.

Peter Alliss

There are now more golf clubs in the
world than Gideon Bibles, more golf
balls than missionaries and, if every
golfer in the world, male and female,
were laid end to end, I for one would
leave them there.

Michael Parkinson

What's over there? A nudist colony?

*Lee Trevino (after his 3 playing partners
drove into the woods)*

Anytime you get the urge to golf, instead take 18 minutes and beat your head against a good solid wall! This is guaranteed to duplicate to a tee the physical and emotional beating you would have suffered playing a round of golf. If 18 minutes aren't enough, go for 27 or 36 - whatever feels right.

Mark Oman

The entire handbook can be reduced to three rules. One: you do not touch your ball from the time you tee it up to the moment you pick it out of the hole. Two: don't bend over when you are in the rough. Three: when you are in the woods, keep clapping your hands.

Charles Price

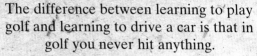

The difference between learning to play
golf and learning to drive a car is that in
golf you never hit anything.

Anon

As of this writing, there are
approximately 2,450 reasons why a
person hits a rotten shot, and more are
being discovered every day.

Jay Cronley

I still swing the way I used to,
but when I look up the ball is going in
a different direction.

Lee Trevino

There's only one thing wrong about
Babe and me. I hit like a girl and
she hits like a man.

Bob Hope
(referring to Babe Didrikson Zaharias)

When ground rules permit a golfer to
improve his lie, he can either move his
ball or change the story about his score.

Anon

Actually, the only time I ever took
out a one-iron was to kill a tarantula.
And I took a seven to do that.

Jim Murray

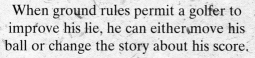

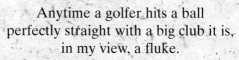

Anytime a golfer hits a ball
perfectly straight with a big club it is,
in my view, a fluke.

Jack Nicklaus

Ah well. If we hit it perfect every day,
everybody else would quit.

Lee Trevino to Tom Watson

Caddies are a breed of their own. If you
shoot a 66, they'll say, 'Man, we shot a
'66!' But go and shoot 77 and they'll say,
'Hell, he shot a 77!'

Lee Trevino

Most golfers prepare for disaster.
A good golfer prepares for success.

Bob Toski

Suffering - ! I've got a hen back home
in Charlotte that can lay an egg
further than that!

*Clayton Heafner, (missing a 3 inch putt to
lose the Oakland Open by one shot)*

I'd like to see the fairways more narrow.
Then everybody would have to play
from the rough, not just me.

Severiano Ballesteros

I visualise hitting the ball as far as
JoAnne Carner, putting like Amy Alcott,
looking like Jan Stephenson and having
Carol Mann's husband.

Dinah Shore

You've got to turn yourself into a
material as soft as putty, and then just
sort of slop the clubhead through.
You'll hit much farther and
with less effort.

Johnny Miller

If ah didn't have these ah'd hit it
twenty yards further.

*Babe Didrikson Zaharias
(referring to her breasts)*

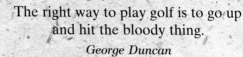

The right way to play golf is to go up
and hit the bloody thing.

George Duncan

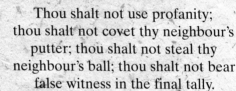

Thou shalt not use profanity;
thou shalt not covet thy neighbour's
putter; thou shalt not steal thy
neighbour's ball; thou shalt not bear
false witness in the final tally.

Ground Rules: Clergyman's Golf Tournament,
Grand Rapids

He quit playing when I started
outdriving him.

JoAnne Carner
(referring to her husband Don)

Real golfers tape The Masters so
they can go play themselves.

George W Roope

Everybody has two swings - a beautiful
practice swing and a choked-up one with
which they hit the ball. So it wouldn't
do either of us a damned bit of good to
look at your practice swing.

Ed Furgol

I don't think that was me that shot that
eighty-four. It must have been somebody
else. Actually, I was trying to get my
handicap squared away.

Fuzzy Zoeller

I only hit the ball about 220 off the tee,
but I can always find it.

Bonnie Lauer

Through years of experience
I have found that air offers less
resistance than dirt.

*Jack Nicklaus explatning why he tees up
the ball so high*

Golf appeals to the idiot in us and the
child . . . Just how childlike golf players
become is proven by their frequent
inability to count past five.

John Updike

I remember being upset once and
telling my Dad I wasn't following
through right, and he replied,
'Nancy, it doesn't make any difference
to a ball what you do after you hit it.'

Nancy Lopez

Golf is a game in which you yell Fore,
shoot six, and write down five.

Paul Harvey

When he gets the ball into a tough place,
that's when he's most relaxed. I think it's
because he has so much experience at it.

Don Christopher (Jack Lemon's caddie)

When a putter is waiting his turn to
hole-out a putt of one or two feet in
length, on which the match hangs at
the last hole, it is of vital importance
that he think of nothing.
At this supreme moment he ought
studiously to fill his mind with vacancy.
He must not even allow himself the
consolation of religion.

Sir Walter Simpson

Well, in plain old English, I'm driving
it bad, chipping bad, putting bad,
and not scoring at all. Other than that,
and the fact I got up this morning,
I guess everything's okay.

Bob Wynn

Keep on hitting it straight until the wee
ball goes in the hall.

James Braid

Golf increases the blood pressure,
ruins the disposition, spoils the digestion,
induces neurasthenia, hurts the eyes,
callouses the hands, ties kinks in the
nervous system, debauches the morals,
drives men to drink or homicide, breaks
up the family, turns the ductless glands
into internal warts, corrodes the
pneumo-gastric nerve, breaks off the
edges of the vertebrae, induces spinal
meningitis and progressive mendacity,
and starts angina pectoris.

Dr. A S Lamb

My caddie had the best answer to that —
'Just to let the other one know it can
be replaced.'

*Larry Nelson explaining why he carried
two putters*

Never give up. If we give up in this
game, we'll give up on life. If you give
up that first time, it's easier to give up
the second, third, and fourth times.

Tom Watson

Confidence builds with successive putts.
The putter, then, is a club designed to hit
the ball partway to the hole,

Rex Lardner

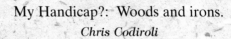

My Handicap?: Woods and irons.

Chris Codiroli

If a ball comes to rest in dangerous proximity to a hippopotamus or crocodile, another ball may be dropped at a safe distance, no nearer the hole, without penalty.

Local Rule: Nyanza Club,
British East Africa in the 1950s

I call my putter 'Sweet Charity' because it covers such a multitude of sins from tee to green.

Billy Casper

Real golfers don't cry when they line
up their fourth putt.

Karen Hurwitz

Players should pick up bomb and shell
splinters from the fairways in order to
save damage to the mowers.

British War Rule

Over the years, I've studied habits of
golfers. I know what to look for. Watch
their eyes. Fear shows up when there
is an enlargement of the pupils.
Big pupils lead to big scores.

Sam Snead

The person I fear most in the last
two rounds is myself.

Tom Watson (at the US Open)

The nice thing about these [golf] books is
that they usually cancel each other out.
One book tells you to keep your eye on
the ball; the next says not to bother.
Personally, in the crowd I play with,
a better idea is to keep your eye
on your partner.

Jim Murray

You've just one problem. You stand too
close to the ball - after you've hit it.

Sam Snead (to a pupil)

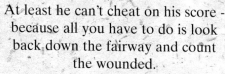

At least he can't cheat on his score -
because all you have to do is look
back down the fairway and count
the wounded.

Bob Hope

He enjoys that perfect peace,
that peace beyond all understanding,
which comes at its maximum only to
the man who has given up golf.

P G Wodehouse

Always throw clubs ahead of you.
That way you don't have to waste energy
going back to pick them up.

Tommy Bolt

The little white ball won't move until you've hit it, and there's nothing you can do after it has gone.

Babe Didrikson Zaharias

The average expert player - if he is lucky - hits six, eight or ten real shots in a round. The rest are good misses.

Tommy Armour

Sure, the purses are obscene. The average worker, let's say, makes $25,000 a year, while a golfer makes $25,000 for finishing 10th. Our values have departed somewhat.

Tom Watson (1989)

True golfers do not play the game
as a form of stress management.
Quite the reverse. They play to establish
superiority over *(a)* themselves,
(b) inanimate objects such as a small
white ball with dimples in it, and
(c) their friends. All of which can
become rather tedious.

Colin Bowles

Play is conducted at a snail's pace.
Some golfers today remind me of kids
walking to school and praying they'll be
late. . . . Golfers used to check the grass
of the greens; today they study the
roots under each blade.

Jimmy Demaret (1954)

I've noticed some of them are off
balance when they swing. They're
top-heavy. They've got too much hair.
Ben Hogan on today's golfers (1970)

I was afraid to move my lips in front
of TV. The Commissioner probably
would have fined me just for what
I was thinking.

Tom Weiskopf
(on his 13 in the 1980 Masters)

It is nothing new or original to say
that golf is played one stroke at a time.
But it took me many years to realise it.

Bobby Jones

Everyone gets wounded in a game of golf. The trick is not to bleed.

Peter Dobereiner

If you try to break the ball to pieces, the sod may fly farther than your shots. You've got to be gentle. Sweet-talk that ball. Make it your friend and it will stay with you a lot longer.

Sam Snead

I always keep a supply of stimulants handy in case I see a snake, which I also keep handy.

W C Fields
(putting whisky in his golf bag)

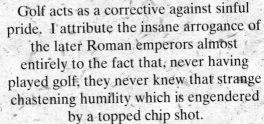

Golf acts as a corrective against sinful pride. I attribute the insane arrogance of the later Roman emperors almost entirely to the fact that, never having played golf, they never knew that strange chastening humility which is engendered by a topped chip shot.

P G Wodehouse

Stroke play is a better test of golf, but match play is a better test of character.

Joe Carr

If you keep shooting par at them, they all crack up sooner or later.

Bobby Jones

A secret disbelief in the enemy's play
is very useful for match play.

Sir Walter Simpson

What the nineteenth hole proves
beyond a shadow of a doubt is that the
Scots invented the game solely in order
to sell their national beverage in
large quantities.

Milton Gross

A good player who is a great putter is a
match for any golfer. A great hitter who
cannot putt is a match for no one.

Ben Sayers

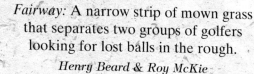

Fairway: A narrow strip of mown grass that separates two groups of golfers looking for lost balls in the rough.

Henry Beard & Roy McKie

No matter what happens - never give up a hole. . . . In tossing in your cards after a bad beginning you also undermine your whole game, because to quit between tee and green is more habit-forming than drinking a highball before breakfast.

Sam Snead

Golf is a typical capitalist lunacy of upper-class Edwardian England.

George Bernard Shaw

If the tree is skinny, aim right at it.
A peculiarity of golf is that what you aim
at you generally miss, ... the success of
the shot depending mainly, of course,
on your definition of 'skinny.'

Rex Lardner

President Ford waits until he hits
his first drive to know what course
he's playing that day.

Bob Hope

When they start hitting back at me,
it's time to quit.

*Henry Ransom (when a shot rebounded from
a cliff and hit him in the stomach)*

Arnold Palmer had everything,
except a brake pedal.

Peter Dobereiner

The fundamental problem with golf
is that every so often, no matter how
lacking you may be in the essential
virtues required of a steady player,
the odds are that one day you will hit the
ball straight, hard and out of sight.
This is the essential frustration of this
excruciating sport. For when you've
done it once, you make the fundamental
error of asking yourself why you can't
do it all the time. The answer to
this question is simple:
the first time was a fluke.

Colin Bowles

A Book of Golfing Quotations

The difference between golf and
government is that in golf you can't
improve your lie.

George Deukmejian (Governor of California)

No man has mastered golf until he has
realised that his good shots are accidents
and his bad shots good exercise.

Eugene R Black

You get to know more of the
character of a man in a round of golf
than you can get to know in six months
with only political experience.

David Lloyd George

Water creates a neurosis in golfers.
The very thought of this harmless fluid
robs them of their normal powers of
rational thought, turns their legs to jelly,
and produces a palsy of the upper limbs.

Peter Dobereiner

The golfer has more enemies than any
other athlete. He has 14 clubs in his bag,
all of them different; 18 holes to play,
all of them different, every week; and all
around him are sand, trees, grass, water,
wind and 143 other players. In addition,
the game is fifty percent mental, so his
biggest enemy is himself.

Dan Jenkins

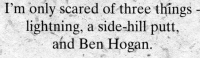

I'm only scared of three things -
lightning, a side-hill putt,
and Ben Hogan.

Sam Snead

The only difference between an amateur
and a pro is that we call a shot that
goes left-to-right a fade and
an amateur calls it a slice.

Peter Jacobsen

Pressure is going out there on the golf
course and thinking, 'If I don't do well,
I'll have to rob another bank.'

Rick Meissner
(former touring pro & convicted bank robber)

I said to the writers, 'There's Nicklaus,
for example, only five strokes back.
I wouldn't feel safe from Jack if
he was in a wheelchair.'

Dan Jenkins

[Tom] Watson scares me. If he's lying six
in the middle of the fairway, there's some
kind of way he might make a five.

Lee Trevino

Hole-in-One: An occurrence in which
a ball is hit directly from the tee
into the hole on a single shot by a
golfer playing alone.

Henry Beard & Roy McKie

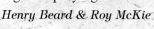

A Book of Golfing Quotations

He hits it in the woods so often he
should get an orange hunting jacket.
Tom Weiskopf on Ben Crenshaw
He goes after a golf course like a lion at
a zebra. He doesn't reason with it;
he tries to throw it out of the window
or hold its head under water till
it stops wriggling.

Jim Murray on Seve Ballesteros

Playing against him [Gary Player],
you begin hoping he'll be on grass rather
than in sand. From grass you expect him
to pitch the ball close. From a bunker
you're afraid he'll hole it out!

Jack Nicklaus

I know I'm getting better at golf
because I'm hitting fewer spectators.

Gerald Ford

The player may experiment about his
swing, his grip, his stance. It is only
when he begins asking his caddie's advice
that he is getting on dangerous ground.

Sir Walter Simpson

If profanity had an influence on the
flight of the ball, the game would be
played far better than it is.

Horace G Hutchinson

In the actual playing of the game,
the golfer cannot keep a great amount of
theory in mind and have any attention
left to bestow upon the ball.

John Dunn

Winning isn't everything,
but wanting to win is.

Arnold Palmer

It is ridiculous to suggest, as some
people do, that golf is a dangerous game.
I myself have only been struck three
times this season!

W T Linskill

What is love compared with holing out
before your opponent?

P G Wodehouse

It is better to smash your clubs than to
lose your temper.

Lord Balfour

If your adversary is a hole or two down,
there is no serious cause for alarm in his
complaining of a severely sprained wrist.
. . . Should he happen to win the next
hole, these symptoms will in all
probability become less troublesome.

Horace G Hutchinson

It's good sportsmanship to not pick up
lost golf balls while they are still rolling.

Mark Twain

Golf is so popular simply because it is
the best game in the world at which to be
bad. .... At golf it is the bad player who
gets the most strokes.

A A Milne

I am quite certain that there has never
been a greater addition to the lighter side
of civilization than that supplied by the
game of golf.

Lord Balfour

Golf is like art;
it's impossible to be perfect.

Sandra Palmer

There are three ways of learning golf:
by study, which is the most wearisome;
by imitation, which is the most fallacious;
and by experience, which is the
most bitter.

Robert Browning

Golfers find it a very trying matter to
turn at the waist, more particularly if
they have a lot of waist to turn.

Harry Vardon

Nobody ever swung the golf club
too slowly.

Bobby Jones

A Scotsman is the only golfer not trying
to hit the ball out of sight.

Anon

The trouble with this game is that they
say the good breaks and bad breaks even
up. What they don't tell you is that they
don't even up right away. You might
go two or three years and all you get is
bad-break bad-break bad-break.
That gets annoying in a hurry.

Johnny Miller

The amateur who picks up his newspaper
and remarks that he could shoot better
golf than those guys on tour should
pause and consider the prospects very
carefully . . . It is not just a different
game. It is not a game at all.

Peter Dobereiner

A golf game doesn't end until the
last putt drops.

Cary Middlecoff

It is a strange thing that we know
just how to do a thing at golf,
and yet we cannot do it.

Bernard Darwin